Original title:

Wandering Sparks Along the Phoenix Knoll

Author: Linda Leevike

ISBN HARDBACK: 978-1-80562-095-2

ISBN PAPERBACK: 978-1-80563-616-8

Flickering Trails of the Endless Sky

Beneath the vault where starlights play,
Whispers of dreams begin to sway.
Paths of fate twinkle and glide,
In the vastness, secrets hide.

Spirits dance on the winds so bold,
Carrying stories yet untold.
A tapestry woven in silver sheen,
Shimmering hopes in the twilight green.

With each heartbeat, the cosmos calls,
Echoes of magic through night's halls.
The flickering trails weave near and far,
Guiding the way, like a distant star.

Ashes Beneath the Twilight Breeze

In the stillness where shadows creep,
Ancient echoes begin to weep.
Beneath the twilight, softly spun,
Ashes whisper of dreams undone.

The last light fades, a fleeting glance,
As shadows waltz in twilight's dance.
Breezes carry tales of yore,
Of love and loss, forevermore.

Crimson skies, a fading glow,
Dance with the memories below.
In every ember, a story lies,
Carried forth on dusk's soft sighs.

Ember Glows in an Open Field

In open fields where fireflies gleam,
Embers flicker like a waking dream.
Night embraces the world in fright,
While whispers twinkle in the night.

A gentle warmth in the cool night air,
Stories rise from the earth laid bare.
Each flicker holds a tale to share,
Of souls intertwined in love's own snare.

Stars above like watchers stand,
In their gaze, the world feels grand.
Embers glow with a patient grace,
Illuminating the darkened space.

Flight of the Scarlet Horizon

Across the sea where the sun sinks low,
Colors blaze in a fiery glow.
Birds of hope take to the skies,
Chasing dreams as daylight dies.

Scarlet horizons beckon and sway,
Guiding hearts on their wondrous way.
With wings of courage, we rise and flee,
In search of what the heart can see.

The twilight calls in a voice so clear,
A promise stitched with threads of cheer.
In every dawn that bids goodbye,
There lies the spark of the endless sky.

The Glow of Promise in Dusk's Embrace

In twilight's soft and gentle light,
Dreams awaken, take their flight.
Whispers of hope dance on the air,
As darkness falls, we find our care.

Stars emerge, shy yet bright,
Guiding us through the fading night.
A promise glows in shadows deep,
Awakening thoughts we long to keep.

The horizon shows a painted sky,
Where wishes linger, soars the sigh.
In dusk's embrace, we find our way,
Towards tomorrow's brand new day.

With every heartbeat, magic stirs,
In the silence, the spirit purrs.
The essence of what's yet to be,
Glow within, forever free.

As night unfolds with velvet grace,
Every soul finds its rightful place.
In the glow of promise, hearts unite,
A tapestry woven with dreams so bright.

Flames of Thought Across the Untamed Land

Across the wild where echoes heed,
Flames of thought ignites the seed.
Visions dance in fire's embrace,
A canvas vast, no time to waste.

Winds of change whisper through trees,
Carrying the scent of ancient keys.
Each flicker tells a story bold,
In untamed lands, new tales unfold.

Through valleys deep and mountains tall,
The flames beckon, resounding call.
Between the shadows, wisdom gleams,
In every flicker, lies our dreams.

As embers spark in twilight's zone,
Thoughts take flight, wild and alone.
In freedom found, our spirits soar,
Through untamed lands, forevermore.

With every blaze, our courage grows,
Filling our hearts with vibrant prose.
Across the fields where wild things roam,
The flames of thought will lead us home.

The Luminous Journey of Lost Souls

In the night where shadows creep,
Lost souls wander, never sleep.
A luminous thread guides the way,
Through darkness, seeking light of day.

Each step taken, a story told,
Of dreams abandoned, hearts turned cold.
Yet glimmers wink from deep inside,
A flicker of hope, none can hide.

Together they roam 'neath starlit skies,
With every quest, their spirits rise.
In fragile glow, they seek their peace,
Longing for bonds that never cease.

Through endless twilight, they will tread,
In kindness shared, all sorrows shed.
For journeys end in where souls mend,
This luminous path knows no end.

So as they wander, hand in hand,
Across the vast and endless land,
Their luminous journey finds a role,
Awakening warmth in every soul.

Rebirth Under Starlit Canopies

Beneath the vast and twinkling dome,
Life awakens, finds its home.
In the hush of night, dreams take wing,
The heart beats loud, begins to sing.

Each star a beacon, glowing bright,
Illuminating paths of night.
Rebirth calls from shadows past,
A dance of spirits, free at last.

In the cool embrace of midnight's glow,
New beginnings start to flow.
Echoes of laughter fill the air,
As hope blooms bright in love's warm care.

With every shimmer, the soul ignites,
Shedding layers of old delights.
Under starlit canopies, we find,
The beauty of being intertwined.

In this sacred space, we shall rise,
Embracing life beyond the skies.
Rebirth under these twinkling lights,
A journey filled with wondrous sights.

Shimmering Footprints in the Night

In the silver glow of the moon,
Footprints trace a whispered tune,
Softly gliding, they depart,
Leaving magic where dreams start.

Stars above begin to sing,
Wings of night on shadowed wing,
Each step tells a tale so bright,
Shimmering softly in the night.

Glimmers dance upon the sea,
Secrets tucked in memory,
The gentle breeze carries a call,
Footprints vanish, one and all.

Yet in the silent, hushed embrace,
Remain the echoes, time and space,
Of moments shared in shadowed light,
In shimmering footprints of the night.

When dawn awakes with blush and grace,
The stories fade, yet leave a trace,
For every dream that slips away,
Holds a luminous ballet.

Flames of Memory on the Hilltop

On a hill where wildflowers grow,
Flames of memory softly glow,
Dancing bright on dusk's embrace,
Painting shadows across the space.

Whispers from the windswept trees,
Tell of days filled with sweet ease,
Each flicker a love, lost and found,
Resounding in the heartbeats' sound.

The horizon pulls the sun so near,
In the warmth, ghosts feel so clear,
Laughter carried on the breeze,
Each flame a cherished memory's tease.

Promises made 'neath a starry sky,
With every flicker, a silent sigh,
On the hill where time stands still,
Flames of memory from the heart spill.

As night falls and colors fade,
The embers twinkle, hopes laid,
In the quiet, they dream, they play,
Flames of memory, never far away.

The Dance of Glowing Shadows

In twilight's hush, they start to play,
Glowing shadows come out to sway,
Beneath the trees, where secrets lie,
They twirl and dip beneath the sky.

With laughter bright, they weave a tale,
Softly drifting like a sail,
Each moment held in gentle grace,
The dance flows swift, time leaves no trace.

Echoes whisper through falling leaves,
In each twirl, the night believes,
Glowing shadows, both fierce and meek,
In the silent language they speak.

Luna's light, their guiding friend,
In this dance that knows no end,
Framing each story, lost and found,
In dancing shadows, joy unbound.

As dawn approaches with golden hue,
The shadows fade, but still feel true,
For every step they took that night,
Holds a spark of lingering light.

Echoes of Light in the Golden Hour

In the golden hour, time slows down,
Light caresses, a cherished crown,
Moments gleam with a gentle grace,
As if the world is a sacred place.

Reflections dance upon the stream,
Radiant whispers of a dream,
Each glimmer holds a story spun,
In the heart of setting sun.

The air is rich with tales untold,
Of laughter shared, and hands to hold,
Every shadow shaped by light,
Becomes a memory, warm and bright.

As day gives way to the night's embrace,
Echoes linger in the silence of space,
And every moment, like a flower,
Blooms in the beauty of the hour.

Though darkness wraps the world in night,
The echoes of light ignite delight,
For in the dusk, where dreams take flight,
We hold on tight to love's pure light.

Fires that Spark and Fade

In whispers of the darkened night,
Fires flicker with a subtle light.
They dance and sway, then fade away,
Leaving shadows where they play.

Each ember holds a memory dear,
A flame that once burned bold and clear.
Yet time will steal their vibrant glow,
And silence where the wild winds blow.

But in their hearts, the stories dwell,
Of warmth and joy, of love to tell.
Though fleeting are the fiery dreams,
They linger still in quiet streams.

So gather 'round, embrace the spark,
Let your laughter light the dark.
For every fire will find its fate,
In ashes, life will still create.

The Dance of Light on the Mountain's Edge

Upon the peaks where eagles soar,
The light performs an ancient lore.
It twists and bends in morning's grace,
A ballet bright in nature's space.

The sun, a painter, bright and bold,
Unfolds a canvas, rich like gold.
From shadowed depths to heights above,
Each ray a whisper, each hue a love.

The mountain holds its breath in awe,
As light spills forth, a golden thaw.
It dances with the wind's sweet song,
In harmony, where hearts belong.

So linger by the mountain's side,
And watch the radiant dreams collide.
For in each step, the light will chase,
A fleeting waltz through time and space.

Flickers of Life in the Forgotten Grove

In the heart of woods, so deep and wide,
Flickers of life in shadows hide.
Bright eyes peep from tangled vines,
In rustling leaves, the magic twines.

The ancient trees with lived-in grace,
Whisper tales of a long-lost place.
Where fairies tread in secret dreams,
And laughter flows in silver streams.

Each glimmer tells a story rare,
Of forgotten lore hung in the air.
So pause and listen to the sighs,
For life awakens where silence lies.

With every step, a breath you take,
Awakens wonders, wild and awake.
In the grove where echoes gleam,
The heartbeat pulses, a timeless dream.

Luminescent Horizons of the Night's Embrace

As dusk descends, the stars ignite,
Luminescent horizons, pure delight.
The moon, a lantern in the sky,
Watches as the dark winds sigh.

Each twinkling light, a distant flame,
Promising dreams that whisper your name.
In night's embrace, all burdens cease,
As shadows mold to realms of peace.

The world transforms in silver hues,
As nighttime weaves her silent muse.
With gentle hands, she cradles hope,
And teaches weary hearts to cope.

So wander forth beneath her gaze,
And let the night unbind your ways.
With every star that lights your flight,
Find solace in the endless night.

Twilight Fragments and Flickering Endings

In twilight's soft embrace, we find,
Fragments of dreams that intertwine.
Shadowed whispers softly call,
As day fades gently, night takes all.

Flickering stars in the darkened skies,
Guide our hearts with their bright sighs.
Moments lost in the fading light,
Promises made in the depth of night.

The moon and sun dance a silent tune,
In the velvet silence, beneath the moon.
Each heartbeat echoes, each breath a sigh,
In this soft twilight, we learn to fly.

Glimmers of hope in the waning glow,
Flickering endings we've come to know.
With every parting, another start,
In the fragile dusk, we hold our heart.

As shadows stretch and the night unfolds,
In twilight's warmth, the brave and bold.
Finding solace in the quiet dark,
We gather our dreams, ignite the spark.

Glimmers in the Depths of the Forest

In the forest deep where shadows lay,
Glimmers of light dance and sway.
Amid the trees, the whispers softly play,
Secrets of the night, come what may.

With each rustling leaf, a tale is spun,
Of ancient magic and the setting sun.
Creatures awaken, with eyes aglow,
In this hallowed realm where wonders flow.

Mossy stones and the rivers bright,
Bathe in the hues of fading light.
Every path winding like a dream,
Leads to glimmers of a lost theme.

In twilight's breath, the forest sighs,
Underneath the watchful, starlit skies.
Glimmers of hope in a hidden glade,
Where fears dissolve in the cool shade.

A dance of shadows, a haunting tune,
In depths of the forest, beneath the moon.
With every step, we lose our way,
Yet find our hearts in the night's ballet.

Visions Made of Sunlight and Shadows

Sunlight spills like golden threads,
Weaving through shadows, gently it spreads.
Visions emerge in the played light,
Guiding the heart, igniting the night.

Whispers of dawn in a world so bright,
Merge with the dark, revealing insight.
Moments captured, in silver beams,
Woven together, like vibrant dreams.

Each shadow dances, each ray does weave,
Stories of hope, we dare believe.
In the silence, a spark ignites,
Where sunlight and shadows embrace their flights.

The twilight beckons with promises vast,
A fusion of futures and echoes of past.
In the interplay of day and night,
Visions are born, taking their flight.

Life's tapestry spun with joy and pain,
With sunlight and shadows as threads we gain.
In this vivid dance, hearts entwined,
A masterpiece emerges, beautifully aligned.

Celestial Migrations of the Wandering Heart

The stars stretch forth like whispers bright,
Celestial paths in the velvet night.
Wandering hearts on a quest divine,
Seeking solace where the heavens shine.

Each comet's tail leaves a fleeting trace,
Of dreams set adrift in the cosmic space.
With every heartbeat, a journey begins,
In the celestial dance, where love transcends.

The moon's soft glow guides the lost souls,
In migrations where destiny unfolds.
A guiding light for those who roam,
In the universe vast, they find their home.

Veils of stardust wrap the weary heart,
Each cycle of passage a brand new start.
With every dusk brings a dawn anew,
In the ballet of stars, light breaks through.

So chase the stars, let your spirit soar,
For in each migration, there's something more.
A heartbeat echoing, vast and free,
In celestial rhythms, we find our key.

Whirling Fires Across Boundless Skies

In the night, the embers dance,
Whirling flames take their stance.
Across the heavens, a carpet glows,
Secrets of the cosmos it bestows.

Flames flicker, shadows glide,
Mysteries in the darkness hide.
The universe sings in fiery delight,
A tapestry woven by stars so bright.

On wings of smoke, the spirits rise,
Carried far beyond worldly ties.
They whisper tales of ancient lore,
Of battles fought and magic more.

Through the air, the sparks will soar,
Kindling dreams we can't ignore.
In this vast and endless night,
Whirling fires spark our inner light.

So gaze upon the starlit sea,
Let your heart wander wild and free.
For in the flames, a truth revealed,
A universe of wonders concealed.

Starlit Dreams on a Silver Wave

Upon the ocean's gentle crest,
Starlit dreams weave and rest.
Silver waves whispering secrets sweet,
A lullaby of nights discreet.

The moon guides ships lost at sea,
Casting shadows that beckon me.
Through the chaos, serenity flows,
In the dance of tides, my spirit glows.

Each ripple carries a wish so bold,
Stories of adventures yet untold.
With every surge, my heart ignites,
In starlit realms, the world delights.

Clouds twirl like dancers in the night,
Embracing the glow of soft moonlight.
I ride the current, wild and free,
In the depths of dreams, I find the key.

So sail with me on this silver ride,
Chasing the starlit tides with pride.
For every dream, a light we crave,
In the embrace of the silver wave.

Streams of Light Through Whispering Pines

Amidst the pines, a soft glow gleams,
Whispers dance on twilight beams.
Streams of light weave through the trees,
Nature sings in a gentle breeze.

The forest breathes, alive and wise,
Guarding secrets beneath the skies.
Each shadow whispers, each leaf replies,
In the embrace of the whispering sighs.

As the moon paints the world in grace,
Mystical paths we long to trace.
In every glimmer, a story unfolds,
In the heart of the woods, the magic holds.

Time slows down, and moments blend,
With every heartbeat, the echoes extend.
Through tangled roots and silver streams,
We wander freely in woven dreams.

So listen closely, and you will find,
In the soft whispers, your heart unwinds.
For in this place, where light aligns,
Enchanting tales bloom in whispering pines.

Mysteries Illuminated in the Silent Woods

In the quiet, where shadows play,
Mysteries beckon, night turns to day.
The woods breathe secrets, ancient and deep,
Guardians of dreams, their vigil keep.

Soft moonlight dapples the forest floor,
Creating magic behind every door.
With gentle steps, we tread the path,
In the silence, we feel its wrath.

Each rustle tells a tale anew,
Of spirits that dwell in the morning dew.
With laughter or sorrow, the echoes roam,
In the heart of the woods, we find our home.

In the stillness, hear nature's song,
A melody haunting yet soothingly strong.
Beneath the canopy, mysteries twine,
In the silent woods, our souls align.

So wander deep, let the magic guide,
Through the veils where hidden truths bide.
For in silence lies the greatest prize,
Mysteries illuminated before our eyes.

The Glowing Tapestry of Old Tales

In shadows deep where legends weave,
Threads of magic, hopes believe.
Colors dance in stories spun,
Whispered tales of all they've done.

Each stitch a moment, secrets shared,
Heroes born, and fates declared.
In threads of gold and silver bright,
Dreams take flight in starry night.

The fabric glows with ancient song,
Echoes of the brave and strong.
Mystic symbols, ages past,
In every pattern, shadows cast.

Glimmers hint at joys and fears,
Silhouettes of lost frontiers.
With every glance, a heart embraced,
In the tapestry, time is traced.

So gather 'round, all young and old,
Let the vibrant stories unfold.
For in this weave, the truth resides,
In every heart, where magic hides.

Flight of the Embered Souls

When twilight falls, the embers rise,
Wings of fire, touching skies.
In the night, where dreams ignite,
Spirits dance in gentle flight.

Through the darkness, bright they roam,
Guided by the stars, their home.
Each heartbeat shines, a flickered spark,
Tracing paths across the dark.

With whispers soft as autumn's breeze,
They carry hopes through swaying trees.
In every flake of ash that flies,
A wish awakens, never dies.

Together bound, they seek the dawn,
In every flame, a love reborn.
Against the chill, they bravely soar,
A symphony forever more.

So when you gaze at evening's glow,
Remember, dear, they still bestow.
A tale of warmth, a heart's embrace,
In embered souls, we find our place.

Beneath the Arch of Flickering Memories

In the twilight, shadows sway,
Hints of moments lost, they play.
Beneath the arch, so grand, so wide,
Echoes linger, joy and pride.

Flickering lights, like stars adorn,
Whispers of a love reborn.
In every crack, a story waits,
Life entangled with fates.

With eyes closed, we travel back,
Through pathways lost, down ancient track.
Each flicker brings a tender sigh,
In memories, we laugh and cry.

So gather near, let shadows take,
The form of dreams that never break.
In every flicker, past entwined,
With every heartbeat, fate designed.

For memories are treasures rare,
Beneath this arch, love fills the air.
In flickering light, we find our way,
Guided by memories that forever stay.

The Enchanted Glade of Lost Dreams

In a glade where wildflowers bloom,
Whispers dwell, and secrets loom.
Shadows dance in twilight's embrace,
Lost dreams linger, find their place.

With every breeze that sweeps the land,
Soft echoes of a guiding hand.
In every petal, memories weep,
In the stillness, silence deep.

Where wishes made on starlit nights,
Have woven magic, held on tight.
With tender threads of hope and fears,
In the glade, all dreams appear.

So lay your heart upon the ground,
For here, the lost are always found.
In mossy beds and sunlight's gleam,
Awakened whispers, lost dreams beam.

With open arms, the glade will greet,
All those who've faced their bitter defeat.
For in this place, with love bestowed,
Upon the path, all dreams are flowed.

The Awakening of Fiery Dreams

In a realm where shadows play,
Whispers stir the night and day.
Flickers dance in twilight's haze,
Fiery dreams begin to blaze.

Stars ignite the velvet skies,
Hope ignites, the heart complies.
In slumber's grip, we dare to soar,
Awakening to dreams galore.

A dance of flames, a spark anew,
Awaits the heart, indulgent view.
In whispered tales of sweet desire,
We nurture all the dreams conspire.

Voices call from realms unseen,
In echoes bright, our souls convene.
With every flicker, truth embraced,
The boundaries blur, forever chased.

So let the fiery visions rise,
Through endless nights and starlit skies.
In dream's embrace, we are alive,
With fiery hearts, we will thrive.

Illumination at the Edge of Time

Amidst the fog of whispered years,
A light emerges from our fears.
At the edge where moments blend,
Illumination, our truest friend.

Time flows like a river wide,
Each wave a glimpse of what's inside.
Through shadows cast by dreams once bold,
A tapestry of memories told.

The clock ticks soft, yet loud it sings,
Each second holds the weight of wings.
In silent pauses, truths unfurl,
Illumination in a swirling world.

The past and future intertwine,
In every heartbeat, you will find.
Glimmers bright on every seam,
A journey steeped in golden dream.

As time unfolds its fragile thread,
With every moment, spirits spread.
Illumination lights our way,
At the edge of night and day.

Bright Paths in the Misty Vale

In the vale where the whispers dwell,
Misty paths weave stories to tell.
Glimmers dance through the shrouded air,
Brightened hopes amidst the despair.

Footprints soft on the dewey ground,
Echoes of dreams, a serenade sound.
Each corner turned, a new surprise,
In the vale, where magic lies.

With every step, the heart feels bold,
Adventures linger, waiting to unfold.
Through veils of mist, a light will gleam,
Guiding souls to a brighter dream.

The stars above begin to wake,
As dawn approaches, the shadows break.
In the vale where we dare to roam,
Bright paths lead us sweetly home.

Nature whispers in vibrant tones,
Among the pines, our spirit roams.
Within the mist, each tale we weave,
A tapestry in which we believe.

Illusive Phenomena on Urban Streets

In the city where shadows blend,
Illusive visions twist and bend.
Streets alive with stories slight,
In the pulse of vibrant night.

Neon signs like stars aglow,
Whisper secrets lovers know.
With every step, a tale unfolds,
In urban streets, where magic holds.

Mirages flicker, dance like fire,
Chasing dreams that never tire.
Echoes of laughter, bittersweet,
Every heartbeat, a rhythmic beat.

Through alleyways and crowded lanes,
Moments linger, hope remains.
Illusions play like shadows cast,
In the tapestry of the fast.

Beneath the glow of midnight's eye,
We search for truth, we aim to fly.
Illusive wonders, capturing hearts,
In the city, where wonder starts.

Radiant Whispers in the Dark

In shadows deep, a secret sighed,
Where dreams entwined, and fears abide.
Soft echoes dance on moonlit streams,
A tale unfolds of shattered dreams.

The nightingale sings a lonesome tune,
Beneath the gaze of a watchful moon.
Stars twinkle bright, like diamonds rare,
They weave their magic through the air.

With every flicker, hope ignites,
Guiding lost souls through sleepless nights.
A spark within, though dimly seen,
Awakens strength where none has been.

Amidst the gloom, a voice appears,
Whispering truths to calm the fears.
Heartbeats quicken, shadows flee,
For even night must yield to glee.

So take the hand of light anew,
Release the dark, find paths so true.
For whispers radiant, once confined,
Shall lead you home, your heart aligned.

Journey Through the Embered Woods

Through rustling leaves, the forest breathes,
Each branch a tale, each root it weaves.
The amber glow of fireflies dance,
Inviting souls to take a chance.

A winding path of whispered lore,
With secrets hidden, forevermore.
Ancient trees with wisdom vast,
Guard memories of ages past.

Footfalls soft on earthy ground,
In every silence, magic found.
Hushed voices beckon from afar,
A guiding light, a distant star.

Where shadows stretch and dark things sway,
Courage blooms along the way.
Within the heart, a fire burns,
Through embered woods, the world returns.

So wander forth, embrace the night,
For hidden wonders lie in sight.
With every step, a spark will surge,
And in your soul, dreams shall emerge.

Flicker of Hope on Distant Peaks

Upon the heights where breezes play,
A flicker shines, both bright and gay.
Like morning dew on blades of grass,
A whisper echoes, dare to pass.

The mountains loom, their majesty grand,
With silent strength, they take a stand.
In daunting heights, dreams oft reside,
With courage, they face the rising tide.

From crags where shadows stretch so wide,
Hope dances lightly, like a bride.
Each heartbeat tells of tales untold,
Of journeys steep and spirits bold.

As clouds embrace the sky above,
A promise sprouts, a fleeting love.
For every struggle faced with grace,
Will find its place in endless space.

So climb, dear heart, to heights unknown,
In every summit, seeds are sown.
A flame ignites, it will not cease,
For in those peaks, we find our peace.

Glimmers Above the Mountain Pass

Through winding trails where shadows linger,
A glimmer shines—a magic singer.
Upon the ridge, a light so fair,
Whispers of winds, they beckon prayer.

The chilly air, it wraps so tight,
But underneath, there's warmth in sight.
A beacon bright, against the gray,
It calls the brave to find their way.

With every step, the heart does race,
As beauty blooms in this wild space.
The pass may steep, the path may twist,
Yet hope persists, it can't be missed.

From heights above, the valleys gleam,
In golden hues, like childhood dreams.
Each glimmer sparks a wish anew,
For in the journey, we pursue.

So take a breath, embrace the climb,
In every moment, feel the time.
The mountain's pass, a sacred trust,
Leads every dreamer, ever just.

Flickers of Hope Amidst the Darkness

In shadows deep where whispers dwell,
A spark arises, casts its spell.
Through trials grim, we dare to weave,
A tapestry of hope, believe.

The night may close, the chill may bite,
Yet flickers shine with tender light.
Each heartbeat strong, each sigh we share,
A flickering flame dispels despair.

In silent woods, where fears reside,
A glimmer guides, a faithful guide.
Though darkness looms, we face the storm,
In unity, our spirits warm.

So gather close when shadows fall,
For within us burns a mighty call.
Together bound, we rise anew,
Our hope ignites, a beacon true.

Twinkling Stars on the Slopes of Fate

Upon the hills where dreams take flight,
Twinkling stars adorn the night.
Each wishes whispered, softly spun,
A dance of fate, our journey begun.

Through valleys low and peaks so high,
The stars above, our constant sky.
In every heart, a story glows,
A guiding light that always knows.

The paths ahead may twist and turn,
Yet in our souls, a fire burns.
With every step, the heavens sing,
Their melodies, a gentle wing.

So lift your gaze, behold the view,
The stars align, they shine for you.
With courage found on fate's vast slate,
Embrace the night; it's never late.

Celestial Fireflies and Dreaming Horizons

In twilight's glow, the fireflies gleam,
With winks of light, they spark a dream.
Across the fields where whispers dance,
They guide our hearts to brave romance.

The horizons call, a bold embrace,
With colors bright, they paint the space.
Each dream we dare, each hope we find,
Is stitched with threads of love, entwined.

Through starlit paths, our laughter flies,
As we chase shadows, beneath the skies.
Together bound, we chase the night,
Celestial fireflies, pure delight.

So seize the stars, let dreams ignite,
In every heartbeat, feel the flight.
With every wish, horizons bloom,
As fireflies chase away the gloom.

Reflections on the Echoing Summit

On distant peaks where echoes play,
Reflections glint in bright array.
The summit calls with silent grace,
A sacred space, a tranquil place.

With every breath, the world unfolds,
A tapestry of tales retold.
The whispers of the ancient trees,
Embrace our hopes like a gentle breeze.

In mirrored depths, our truths reside,
As we traverse the mountainside.
Each challenge met, each sorrow faced,
Becomes a verse of dreams embraced.

So up we climb, with hearts so bold,
In every stride, our dreams take hold.
The summit waits, a promise dear,
In echoes soft, we shall persevere.

A Tale Woven in Radiance

In a garden where whispers play,
The flowers bloom in bright array,
A tale unfolds beneath the sun,
With golden threads, our hearts are spun.

Magic dances in the light,
Casting shadows, pure and bright,
Each petal tells a story true,
Of dreams that spark like morning dew.

Among the leaves, a songbird sings,
Of distant lands and painted wings,
A woven path through time and space,
In its melody, we find our place.

The sun dips low, a gentle sigh,
As twilight paints the evening sky,
With colors bold and soft embrace,
We rest our thoughts in nature's grace.

As stars appear, the tales grow wide,
The night reveals what hearts can't hide,
A tapestry of hopes and dreams,
That glimmers bright as starlight beams.

Dreams of Light Beneath the Silent Stars

Beneath the stars, in velvet night,
Whispers of dreams take their flight,
The moon, a guardian in the sky,
Beckons souls to wander by.

In the silence, shadows play,
Dancing hopes that drift away,
Each twinkle tells a tale untold,
Of wishes cast, both brave and bold.

Across the vast, enchanted sea,
The light that calls, a melody,
With every wave, a spark ignites,
In dreams of love on starry nights.

From sleepy towns to mountains high,
The echoes of our laughter fly,
A symphony of hearts so rare,
In every breath, a wish laid bare.

So when the dawn begins to rise,
And paints the world with golden skies,
Remember well the night's sweet charms,
For dreams of light still wait in arms.

The Light that Beckons from Afar

A lantern glows on yonder hill,
Its gentle warmth, a calming thrill,
With every flicker, tales are spun,
Of journeys bright and races run.

Through misty paths where shadows hide,
The beckoning light, a faithful guide,
With whispers soft like evening breeze,
It calls to hearts that long for ease.

Adventurous souls seek to explore,
The vale beyond, where memories soar,
In the light's embrace, they find their way,
Through tangled woods and skies of gray.

Beneath the vast, eternal sky,
Stars weave tales that never die,
And every glimmer, every hue,
Is a promise shared, forever true.

So follow the light, let it lead,
To places where our spirits feed,
In the luminous glow of love and dreams,
Life is richer than it seems.

Dusk's Embrace in Celestial Journeys

As dusk descends with velvet touch,
The world exhales, it feels so much,
In twilight's arms, we drift and sway,
Our hopes and fears in soft decay.

Cascading colors brush the night,
An artist's hand, a pure delight,
Each stroke a whisper, a gentle plea,
To guide our hearts, to set them free.

Among the stars, our dreams take flight,
On currents borne of endless night,
The cosmic dance, a splendid show,
A tapestry of what we know.

In every heartbeat, time suspends,
As night reveals the truth it lends,
So gather close, with arms entwined,
In dusk's embrace, our souls aligned.

For every journey that we face,
Is filled with light, and love's sweet grace,
Together we shall weave and wander,
In celestial dreams, forever fonder.

Mysterious Whirls in Celestial Currents

In the night sky, stars dance bright,
Whispers of dreams take flight.
Galaxies spinning, secrets untold,
A tapestry of wonders unfolds.

Comets streak like fleeting thoughts,
In the silence, the cosmos caught.
Each twinkle, a story of old,
In mysteries, our hearts are sold.

Nebulas bloom in hues so rare,
A canvas painted with cosmic care.
In their depths, we seek our place,
Amongst the wonders of time and space.

Rippling currents of time entwined,
In the folds of space, we seek to find.
A journey through realms, both dark and light,
In mysterious whirls, we take flight.

With every gaze at the night's embrace,
We unravel shadows time cannot trace.
In celestial currents, we lose our fears,
And dance with the stars through the years.

Shimmers of Eternity in Wandering Minds

Dreams weave softly through the night,
Casting shadows, dancing light.
In wandering minds, secrets dwell,
Echoes of stories we long to tell.

Upon the path of thought's sweet grace,
We meet the echoes of a familiar face.
Illuminated visions, bright and bold,
Whispers of wisdom in silence unfold.

Time flows gently, like a stream,
Lost in the passage, we float and dream.
Shimmers of eternity flash and gleam,
In the fabric of our inner theme.

Memories linger, tender, clear,
In the maze of moments we hold dear.
With every heartbeat, the journey starts,
In the flicker of light, we find our hearts.

Through the labyrinth of fate's design,
We gather stories, our souls entwined.
In wandering minds, forever roam,
For within our thoughts, we find our home.

Phantoms of Radiance in the Winding Woods

In the heart of the woods, shadows play,
Phantoms of radiance drift away.
With every rustle, an echo sings,
The magic of twilight on glowing wings.

Moonlight filters through branches high,
Dancing softly in the midnight sky.
A symphony of whispers, sweet and low,
In the winding woods where the wild dreams grow.

Footsteps echo on a path unseen,
Secrets woven in the spaces between.
The pulse of the forest, alive and real,
In every heartbeat, the world we feel.

With each step deeper, the stars align,
In the embrace of shadows, we intertwine.
A spectacle of wonder, hidden from sight,
Phantoms of radiance, embracing the night.

In this sanctuary, spirits thrive,
Where the essence of nature comes alive.
Through winding paths, we wander and play,
In the hands of magic, we long to stay.

The Ethereal Glow of Untamed Thoughts

Untamed thoughts flicker like flames,
In baskets woven from dreams and names.
An ethereal glow lights the dark,
Igniting the imagination's spark.

Whispers of ideas drift through the air,
Daring to dream, free from care.
In the silence of night, they swirl and twist,
In the labyrinth of minds, they quietly exist.

Thoughts like fireflies dance in a trance,
Yearning for freedom, eager to prance.
Caught in the ether, alive and bright,
The pulse of creation ignites the night.

Each flicker of thought, a rare delight,
Giving birth to worlds in the veil of night.
In the realm of wonder, we explore and seek,
For in untamed thoughts, our spirits speak.

Together we wander, lost in the flow,
Sculpting the future from visions aglow.
With each gentle breeze, new dreams take flight,
In the ethereal glow, we chase the light.

Dance of Light and Mist on Fragrant Winds

In twilight's embrace, the soft shadows sway,
Where whispers of dew greet the dawning day.
With petals aglow, they shimmer and spin,
A waltz of the wild, where dreams dare to begin.

The breeze carries songs from the trees far and wide,
While secrets of nature in rhythm abide.
Through dappled light, the flowers all twirl,
An enchanting ballet in a mystical whirl.

The clouds weave their tales as the sun dips low,
In a dance of gold where the waters flow.
Every shimmer and sparkle, a story unfolds,
Of moments in time, worth more than their gold.

As echoes of laughter and joy intertwine,
In this garden of magic, where hearts align.
With each gentle footstep on soft, verdant grass,
We waltz with the cosmos, let the magic amass.

So linger a while, let your spirit take flight,
In the dance of the day turning soft into night.
For in this sweet realm where the fragrant winds blow,
The dance of our dreams paints the world with a glow.

Land of Flickering Spirits and Winding Paths

In the land where whispers of twilight reside,
Flickering spirits in shadows abide.
They drift through the trees and dance on the breeze,
With secrets and laughter that echo like seas.

Winding paths beckon with stories untold,
Through meadows of silver and valleys of gold.
Each step leads us deeper where wonders are spun,
In the land of the spirited, where magic begun.

With lanterns aglow, they guide us with light,
Through twists and through turns in the heart of the night.

Where laughter is timeless, and sorrows unmade,
In the glow of their warmth, all shadows do fade.

As starlight adorns every leaf and each stone,
The spirits remind us we're never alone.
In this mystical realm where dreams intertwine,
We discover the beauty of paths we design.

So journey with me, through this ethereal gleam,
In the land of the flickering, chase every dream.
For each winding path leads us further within,
To the heart of the magic where our tales may begin.

Celestial Journeys Through Forgotten Realities

In the murmurs of night where the stars softly gleam,
We embark on a voyage, a magical dream.
Through realms of forgotten, where shadows take flight,
In celestial journeys, we dance with the night.

Each twinkling star tells of stories long past,
Of kingdoms and wonders that ever shall last.
They flicker like memories, lost in the air,
Inviting us gently to wander somewhere.

As comets blaze trails in the stillness of space,
We traverse through dimensions, a ethereal chase.
In the fabric of time, we weave through the dark,
Chasing dreams of the universe, igniting our spark.

Beyond the horizon where mysteries hide,
In whispers of galaxies, we choose to abide.
With eyes wide open, we find our own way,
Through celestial realms where our spirits can play.

So take my hand softly, let's float through the skies,
In journeys of wonder, where magic never dies.
For in every heartbeat, a universe blooms,
In celestial realms, we find respite's sweet tunes.

Flickers and Glows: A Battle of the Mind

In the theater of thought, where shadows collide,
Flickers and glows make our choices decide.
With whispers of doubt and the echoes of fear,
A battle of minds, as our visions draw near.

The flickers of hope fight the darkness within,
With bursts of bright strength, they help us begin.
Yet doubts cast their shadows, like clouds on the sun,
In this war for our spirits, who shall overcome?

With courage, we stand on this fragile tightrope,
As thoughts dance around us, igniting our hopes.
In flashes of brilliance, our truths come alive,
In this vivid arena, our dreams will survive.

For each flicker of doubt, a glow will respond,
In the depths of our minds, a vast light will bond.
It's a duel of ideas, a spark to ignite,
As we fiercely create in the soft velvet night.

So rise, dear dreamer, let your will be the guide,
Through the flickers and glows, let your spirit reside.
In the battle of minds, let your heart lead the way,
For the brightest of stars were born from dismay.

Illuminated Paths of the Awakening Dawn

As daybreak spills on hills so high,
Awakening dreams breathe soft and shy.
Morning dew glimmers on leaves so green,
Nature stirs gently, a tranquil scene.

Voices of birds weave tales anew,
Each note a promise, bold and true.
Winds whisper secrets, unbroken grace,
Guiding lost souls to a sacred place.

In the heart of the forest, shadows play,
Meandering trails that beckon and sway.
Footsteps in rhythm with the earth's beat,
Life reawakens, a spirit to greet.

Golden rays pierce the misty veil,
Lighting the journey, a wondrous tale.
With every sunrise, hope finds its way,
Illuminated paths welcome the day.

Soaring Whispers Below the Celestial Crown

Underneath the stars, dreams take flight,
Galaxies swirl in the velvet night.
Silver beams dance on the ocean's face,
Whispers of magic, a tranquil grace.

Mountains stand tall, guardians of lore,
Their ancient stories make spirits soar.
Moonlight cascades in a shimmering stream,
Binding the world in a silvery dream.

Crickets serenade the dusk with delight,
Marking the passage from day into night.
Each twinkling star bears a secret wish,
In the canvas of heaven, all hearts can miss.

A compass of light guides the lost and the bold,
Carving the tales that have yet to be told.
Breathless horizons, where passion resides,
Soaring whispers carry on celestial tides.

Radiant Dances Underneath the Aether

In the realm where daydreams play,
Light pirouettes in a magical ballet.
Colors collide in a vibrant embrace,
Radiant dances unfold in space.

With every twirl, stories come alive,
Sparks of imagination, daring to strive.
The sun and the moon in a tender waltz,
Join hands in harmony, breaking all vaults.

Winds carry laughter, soft and bright,
As petals cascade in the warm twilight.
Echoes of joy ripple through the trees,
Whispering secrets on a gentle breeze.

Time stands still, in a moment divine,
Where hearts unite in rhythm and rhyme.
Stepping in time with the universe's art,
Radiant dances awaken the heart.

The Alchemy of Light and Shadows

In twilight's embrace, a spell unfolds,
Where essence of light and dark gently molds.
Shadows stretch like fingers in play,
Crafting the magic that guides our way.

Echoes of twilight, hush and refine,
Merging the realms of the divine.
The sun dips low, casting tales untold,
Whispers of mystery in colors bold.

Glimmers of starlight begin to ignite,
Shimmering jewels of the deepening night.
Every flicker tells of what's concealed,
In the dance of our lives, truth is revealed.

Hold onto the moments where light meets dusk,
In the spaces between, find the magic we trust.
For in the alchemy that shadows sow,
We discover the light that forever will glow.

Celestial Flames and Distant Shores

In the night, stars whisper low,
Guiding dreams where shadows flow,
Waves come crashing on the sand,
A dance of light, so vast and grand.

Below the sky, so deep, so wide,
Hearts are carried by the tide,
Celestial flames, they flicker bright,
Drawing souls into the night.

As the moon casts silver glow,
Secrets of the ancients show,
Footprints lead to whispered tales,
On distant shores, where love prevails.

In twilight's grasp, the echoes wane,
Yet each memory sings of gain,
Through the mist, hope's gentle call,
Embraces us, lest we should fall.

The night unfolds its velvet hue,
Painting dreams in every view,
Celestial flames guide the brave,
On distant shores, they seek and save.

Twilight Illuminated by Hidden Beauty

In twilight's cloak, the world transforms,
A tender hush as night adorns,
With colors soft, the edges fade,
Hidden beauty in the shade.

Beneath the sky, the shadows dance,
The stars awaken, take their chance,
Whispers float on gentle breeze,
Carrying secrets through the trees.

Each moment shines, though fleeting fast,
A fragile glow, forever cast,
Illuminated by the heart,
Where all the darkest fears depart.

In corners soft, where silence dwells,
The magic of the twilight swells,
With every breath, the world anew,
In hidden beauty, dreams break through.

So linger here, where time suspends,
In twilight's arms, where journey ends,
Illuminate the paths we find,
With hidden beauty intertwined.

Resonant Echoes of Forgotten Fire

Beneath the ashes, embers sigh,
A whisper of the flames that die,
Yet in the silence, echoes hum,
Resonant songs from what has come.

The forest breathes a gentle tune,
Remnants linger of the moon,
Where shadows stretch, and time stands still,
Forgotten fire with patient will.

In every leaf, a story told,
Of battles brave and spirits bold,
The night recalls, though dreams may fade,
Resonant echoes serenade.

Through winding paths and hidden glades,
The past entwines, no debt evades,
A flicker calls from deep within,
Awakens hope where loss has been.

So listen close, let visions spark,
As whispers guide us through the dark,
Resonant echoes, hold the key,
To kindle light in hearts set free.

Flickers on the Edge of Dawn

A hint of gold begins to rise,
Breaking softly through the skies,
Flickers dance on morning's breath,
Awakening the world from death.

In stillness waits a dream unbent,
The promise wrapped in wonderment,
Past the horizon, life will bloom,
With flickers bright, dispelling gloom.

Every heartbeat, every sigh,
Marks the passage of time nearby,
A canvas stretched in pastel hues,
As dawn unveils the day's debut.

Hope ignites with every ray,
Chasing shadows far away,
Flickers weave through trees and air,
A symphony beyond compare.

So let your spirit rise and sing,
With the dawn, new life will spring,
Flickers on the edge of fate,
Awake and witness love create.

The Dance of Shadows in the Light

In the glimmer where dreams align,
Flickers of gold and shadows entwine.
Whispers of magic, soft as a sigh,
Dancing together, they twirl and fly.

Under the moon, where secrets reside,
The shadows frolic, taking their stride.
In every corner, a story unfolds,
Of wonder and whimsy, of truths untold.

Joyful and solemn, they spin in delight,
Painting the canvas of deep velvet night.
In the heartbeat of time, they softly sway,
A dance of the night, a grand cabaret.

Through flickering candle, their forms glide near,
Encapsulating dreams, banishing fear.
In this ballet of light and of shade,
Each step they take, a promise is made.

So linger awhile, in this spellbinding trance,
Where shadows and light forever shall dance.
For in this embrace of twilight's grace,
Magic whispers secrets, the world's warm embrace.

Trails of Thought in Luminous Veils

Amidst the starlight, thoughts softly flow,
Veils of insight, a delicate glow.
Every shimmering thread spins a tale,
Woven in whispers, on soft, gentle gales.

Through ethereal mists, the mind takes flight,
Chasing the wonders of day into night.
Trails of reflections, so vivid, so clear,
Carved in the silence, each one we hold dear.

Each thought a beacon, each spark a refrain,
Echoes of laughter, and moments of pain.
They flutter like moths to the flame of the mind,
Guiding our journeys, their gifts intertwined.

The currents of knowledge, they sweep us along,
In radiant, weaving, an intricate song.
For within these veils of luminous sheen,
We find the truth in the spaces between.

So dance with your thoughts in the gathering light,
With trails of imagination, take off in flight.
Embrace the shadows, let visions unfurl,
Luminous veils, our hearts they will whirl.

Silent Echoes of the Night's Flame

In the hush of the dark, where time stands still,
Silent echoes linger, weaving their will.
Whispers of ember, aglow in the night,
Stories forgotten, igniting their light.

Beneath the broad sky, where starlight will gleam,
The night's gentle flame fuels every dream.
In the quietest corners, secrets take flight,
With rustling leaves, in the arms of the night.

Each flicker, a memory, captured in glow,
A tapestry woven of joy and of woe.
They dance in the stillness, a ghostly ballet,
Echoes of dreams that the darkness won't fray.

Lost in the twilight, where shadows conspire,
The night's flame illuminates hearts that aspire.
To chase after wishes, to conquer the fear,
And find in the silence the truths we hold dear.

So linger a moment, in night's warm embrace,
Hear the echoes, each whisper, each trace.
For in this cocoon, where shadows do play,
The silent night's flame guides our hearts on their way.

The Glow of Memories in the Twilight Realm

In twilight's embrace, where day meets the night,
Memories shimmer, soft whispers take flight.
The glow of the past bathes the world in gold,
Tales of affection, of laughter retold.

Beneath the soft glow, each moment we keep,
Drifting like bubbles in memories deep.
They dance in the air, casting light on our way,
Guiding our journeys through each fleeting day.

In the realm of remembrance, shadows entwine,
Threads of connection in patterns divine.
With each breath, we breathe life into dreams,
In the canvas of twilight, nothing's as it seems.

So treasure the glow of the moments you find,
Let go of the past, to the future be kind.
For memories linger, verdant and bright,
In the twilight's soft glow, they weave day into night.

In this wondrous domain, where hope's gently sown,
The glow of our memories assures we're not alone.
With each fleeting second, let love softly reel,
In the twilight's embrace, let our hearts gently heal.

The Shimmering Ribbons of Existence

In the dawn's soft glow, they dance and weave,
Threads of possibility, one can hardly perceive.
Woven through time, with whispers so light,
Each shimmer of fate, in the morning so bright.

Ghosts of lost dreams, entwined in a flow,
A tapestry grand, where shadows may glow.
With laughter and tears, they flutter and play,
Reminding us gently of what slips away.

A flicker of hope, in this fragile strand,
Carving our paths with a delicate hand.
Ebbing and flowing, like waves on the shore,
These ribbons of life, forever explore.

In moments of silence, their beauty takes flight,
Connecting our souls through the veil of the night.
As colors collide in the vast twilight sky,
These shimmering ribbons weave secrets on high.

Holding the dreams of the ones yet to be,
The shimmering strands, like the depths of the sea.
A map of our hearts, in its depths, we dive,
Through wondrous existence, we truly arrive.

Trails of Light Embracing Ethereal Spaces

Across the dark canvas, light threads unfurl,
Painting the silence with whispers that swirl.
Each beacon, a promise, each ray, a soft sigh,
Guiding the wanderers under the night sky.

With laughter of stars, the cosmos does sing,
As trails of bright lumens to dreamers take wing.
They shimmer like diamonds on velvet so deep,
In this embrace of the light, we shall leap.

Ethereal pathways entwined in pure grace,
Carving the wonders of infinite space.
In the dance of the night, where shadows do play,
We chase the last echoes of twilight's decay.

Each flicker a story from eons ago,
The trails of soft light in a luminous flow.
With visions unbound, into brilliance we tread,
In the heart of the cosmos, where dreams are bred.

So let your heart soar where the trails converge,
Amongst stars and stories, let your spirit surge.
For within these bright pathways, our spirits unite,
Embracing the magic of ethereal light.

Celestial Flickers Between Dreaming Trees

In the whispering woods, where the shadows reside,
Celestial flickers of dreams often glide.
Like fireflies dancing in soft evening's glow,
The magic of starlight begins its sweet show.

Beneath the tall trees, where secrets are spun,
The flickers of light weave tales to be won.
Each shimmer a promise, a wish set afloat,
In the heart of the night, where our dreams oft emote.

With leaves brushing softly, the melody hums,
As celestial whispers entice curious drums.
Through branches and skies, ancient stories take flight,
In the flickers of magic that bloom in the night.

With every soft breeze, a new tale begins,
In the heart of the forest where time always spins.
These flickers unite us, both lost and we found,
In the cradle of dreams, our souls intertwound.

So let us embark on this journey tonight,
With the flickers as lanterns, leading us right.
For between dreaming trees, under midnight's embrace,
We find the true essence of time and of space.

Threads of Glow in the Cosmic Tapestry

In the fabric of night, stars weave their song,
Each twinkle a thread, where dreams belong.
A tapestry dance, of light and of fate,
Woven by hands of a time still innate.

Galaxies swirl in a cosmic embrace,
Whispers of wonders reside in their grace.
A flicker of hope in the vastness of space,
Guiding lost hearts to their rightful place.

The moon casts a glow on horizons unseen,
Illuminating paths where the shadows have been.
Threads of connection, a delicate weave,
Binding our journeys, in what we believe.

Each moment a bead on the string of the hours,
Blooming like night blooms, revealing their powers.
Through the darkest of times, the light will abide,
In the threads of the cosmos, our dreams will reside.

Whispers of Light on the Breath of Dawn

When twilight surrenders to dawn's gentle call,
The whispers of light begin to enthrall.
As the night bids farewell with a soft, tender sigh,
New hues of existence awaken the sky.

A canvas of pastel in soft shades unfurled,
Restoring lost hopes to a waiting world.
Each ray a reminder of dreams yet to chase,
The breath of the day carries grace to embrace.

The dew-kissed petals shimmer with flame,
Each drop a promise, never the same.
The song of the morn dances through every tree,
A symphony waking, forever free.

In the arms of the dawn, all fears melt away,
With whispers of hope guiding the way.
As light overcomes what the night tried to claim,
A promise to rise, and never the same.

The Unseen Path of Forgotten Trails

In the heart of the forest, where shadows entwine,
The path lies in silence, a secret divine.
Overgrown thickets and whispers of yore,
Echo the journeys that came before.

With each step we take on this winding spree,
The past softly beckons, a ghost we can see.
Faint echoes of laughter, the rustle of leaves,
The memories linger like dust on the eaves.

Through the maze of the dusk, we wander so free,
Past trails of the ancients, their stories to see.
The unseen guides us, in shadows unfold,
Treasures of wisdom, experiences told.

Where dreams intertwine with the fabric of space,
A journey transcending time and its grace.
Each step a connection, both lost and profound,
On the unseen path, new light can be found.

Illuminate the Dreams Beneath the Stars

Under a blanket of shimmering night,
Dreams dance in the shadows, igniting the light.
The stars are our guardians, watchful and bright,
Illuminating wishes that glimmer in flight.

In the stillness of dark, there's magic to find,
As hopes intertwine with the cosmos aligned.
Each twinkle a promise, a story to share,
Echoing softly, a song spun with care.

Through valleys of whispers, in galaxies clear,
The weight of our troubles begins to disappear.
With every pulsating glow that we see,
A reminder that dreams are as wild as the sea.

So let us not linger in doubt or despair,
For the universe holds us with tenderest care.
In the silence of night, we'll plant seeds of light,
And watch as our dreams take to wondrous flight.

Flickering Trails in the Twilight Breeze

In the dusk where shadows play,
The flickers dance and softly sway.
Whispers laugh on silken streams,
Chasing the echoes of our dreams.

Winds of magic weave between,
The twilight's veil, a gentle sheen.
Footsteps light as starlit fate,
Guide us where the night is great.

On the path, the fireflies hum,
Each flicker sings of coming fun.
A trail of light, so bright and clear,
Leading hearts that shed their fear.

With every breath, the night unfolds,
Stories of courage, yet untold.
So follow the glow, oh wandering soul,
For love and hope will make you whole.

As the twilight deepens its embrace,
We find our strength, we find our place.
For in this dance of light and gloom,
A brighter dawn will surely bloom.

Echoes of Embered Flight

Across the sky, the embers soar,
Carving paths to distant shores.
Each spark a tale of courage born,
In hearts of those who brave the storm.

With wings of fire, they take their flight,
Chasing dreams in the midnight light.
Echoes ring in the silent night,
Resounding with joy, a pure delight.

Stories etched in the starlit weave,
Of gallant hearts that dare believe.
From shadows cast, a brilliance grows,
In every ember, the magic flows.

So let the flames of hope ignite,
The paths we tread with day and night.
For in each flicker, a promise lies,
And every end brings a new arise.

Through the ashes, we rise anew,
With every challenge, our spirits grew.
In the echoes of the flights we trace,
We find our strength in this embrace.

Glimmers Over the Rising Horizon

When dawn awakes the gentle earth,
A symphony of hope and mirth.
Glimmers shimmer, breaking through,
Painting skies in vibrant hue.

Upon the cusp of day's new light,
Promises bloom, banishing night.
Every whisper, every call,
Sings of love that conquers all.

With open arms, the sun ascends,
Lighting paths where journey bends.
In the warmth, our spirits soar,
Finding treasures on the shore.

Mirrored dreams on the ocean's crest,
In each wave lies a sacred quest.
Chasing glimmers, we stand bold,
For the stories yet untold.

As horizons stretch, embrace the new,
With every heartbeat, brave and true.
Together, we'll face the song of time,
In glimmers bright, our souls will climb.

Ashes Whispering in the Wind

In the quiet, where embers fade,
Ashes whisper of memories made.
Carried softly on the breeze,
Tales of love that time won't seize.

From the ruins, new blooms arise,
In the heart where hope still lies.
Fragile dreams like petals fall,
Remind us that we can stand tall.

Through the echoes of the past,
Lessons learned are meant to last.
In the silence, we find our way,
Guided by the light of day.

So gather close, the stories shared,
In every spark, a soul prepared.
Though ashes may drift and fly,
In our hearts, their spirits lie.

For in the end, it's clear to see,
What once was lost is meant to be.
As whispers rise on the gentle wind,
A new beginning shall rescind.

Celestial Radiance upon Forgotten Trails

Underneath the twilight's veil,
Stars like whispers gently sail.
Footsteps echo on the ground,
Lost in dreams where hope is found.

Moonlit paths weave tales of old,
Stories hidden, yet untold.
In the shadows, secrets cling,
Softly rustling, night birds sing.

Through the mist where laughter fades,
Mysterious and silent shades.
Guiding lights from skies above,
Shimmer softly, like lost love.

Wanderers tread with hearts aglow,
Following where the starlights show.
With each step, a wish takes flight,
Bound by dreams that span the night.

In the distance, echoes soar,
Whispers beckon from the shore.
Celestial sparkles dance and weave,
On forgotten trails, we believe.

Distant Flickers of a Tired Heart

In the depths where shadows dwell,
A heart beats slow, a fading bell.
Memories flicker, dimly bright,
Guiding me through endless night.

Softly, like the dust of time,
Whispers flow in gentle rhyme.
Each fond thought a feathery thread,
Binding life to dreams long fled.

Longing echoes through the air,
Tired soul seeking to repair.
In distant corners, sparks remain,
Lighting paths of joy and pain.

Yet amidst the quiet sighs,
Hope arises, gently flies.
Distant flickers, brave and bold,
Whisper secrets to the cold.

Through the mist, the heart will learn,
From the ashes, souls can burn.
Though weary, we still find a way,
To chase the light of yet-to-day.

Pockets of Light in the Hazy Dawn

In the haze of morning's breath,
Whispers dance, defying death.
Pockets of light begin to flow,
Glistening softly, like fresh snow.

Through branches, sunbeams peek,
Chasing shadows, soft and meek.
Every ray a gentle kiss,
Filling moments with pure bliss.

Here the dreams of night retreat,
As dawn unveils her golden sheet.
In the quiet, magic stirs,
Life awakens, and vision blurs.

Hope unfurls in pastel shades,
Breaking through the night's cool glades.
In each corner of the day,
Pockets of light, come what may.

As the world begins anew,
Chasing phantoms, bright and true.
In this dance of light and dawn,
All forgotten fears are gone.

Glowing Spirits of the Ancient Vale

In the vale where old trees sway,
Whispers of the past still play.
Glowing spirits roam the night,
Guardians of forgotten light.

Through the mist, they softly glide,
Carry dreams on moonlit tide.
Ancient songs in shadows sing,
Promises the twilight brings.

In the depths of emerald glades,
Mysteries entwined in shades.
Flickering forms beneath the sky,
Where echoes of the lost sigh.

Through the ages, they have danced,
In the quiet, we are entranced.
Each soft glow a tale retold,
In the vale where hearts are bold.

Upon the breeze, their laughter sounds,
In every corner, magic bounds.
Glowing spirits, ever near,
In ancient vale, we hold them dear.

www.ingramcontent.com/pod-product-compliance
Ingram Content Group UK Ltd.
Pitfield, Milton Keynes, MK11 3LW, UK
UKHW021443280125

4335UKWH00035B/364

9 781805 636168